LOVE MUSINGS

HENAL CHOKSHI

© Henal Chokshi 2023

All rights reserved by the author. No part of this publication may be reproduced, stored in a retrieval system, or transmitted in any form or by any means, electronic, mechanical, photocopying, recording, or otherwise, without the prior permission of the author.

Although every precaution has been taken to verify the accuracy of the information contained herein, the author and publisher assume no responsibility for any errors or omissions. No liability is assumed for damages that may result from the use of the information contained within.

Title: Love Musings
Language: English
Character set encoding: UTF-8

First published by

An Imprint of BlueRose Publishers

Head Office: B-6, 2nd Floor,
ABL Workspaces, Block B, Sector 4,
Noida, Uttar Pradesh 201301
M: +91-8882 898 898

Dedication

To The Universe,
For We Are All Connected

Acknowledgements

'If the only prayer you said in your whole life was Thank you, that would suffice'

- Meister Eckhart

To Lord Shiva, My Family and Friends.

To the wonderful and exceptional work of all the artists whose music has inspired me to write this book:

As We Keep Searching

Frank Walker

Módl

James Young

Surf Mesa feat. Emilee

Barnes Blvd & Tanerélle

Shallou

Peter Katz

Christopher Bear

Konoba Feat. R. O

Aime Simon (Harry Styles Cover)
Jason Mraz
Sasha Sloan
Henry Green
José González
Pablo Nouvelle
Pablo Nouvelle feat. Lulu James
Pablo Nouvelle feat. Rio
Pablo Nouvelle feat. James Gruntz
Phil Wickham
Tauren Wells
Gorillaz Chase Eagleson
Harry Styles (Loop Cover by Loopink)
Singh Kaur
Matthew Barber
Dave Matthews Band

Preface

Welcome to *Love Musings*. As the author of this collection, I am delighted to share these beautiful expressions of love with you. Each verse in this book holds a special place in my heart, as they are inspired by real emotions. Through these verses, I seek to explore the depths of love's many facets, from the exhilaration of new romance to the hope of finding it in unexpected places. I hope that these poems resonate with you, capturing the essence of your own love stories and touching your soul in profound ways.

Prologue

Through the following pages, I invite you to step into a realm of a new experience combining two art forms: Music and Stories.

At this stage it is advisable to set your music on (earphones / speakers recommended). At the start of each verse, on the top you will see the name of a song and its artist. It is recommended to open this song on your choice of music platform (for example: YouTube/Soundcloud/Spotify etc.)

Once you're into the song for roughly a minute, let's now savour the poetic verses. Let these opening music songs be your guide, as we embark on a journey of melodies and emotions, traversing the landscapes of love, and immersing ourselves in the language of the heart. Enjoy the whole song, while letting your mind exhilarate on each verse.

Contents

COPYRIGHT DECLARATION	II
DEDICATION	V
ACKNOWLEDGEMENTS	VII
PREFACE	XI
PROLOGUE	XIII
CHAPTER 1 EXPERIENCE	19
CHAPTER 2 FEELING	21
CHAPTER 3 MOMENTS	23
CHAPTER 4 INSTINCTS	25
CHAPTER 5 CHOSEN	27
CHAPTER 6 THE WAIT	29
CHAPTER 7 LONGING	31
CHAPTER 8 STORY	33

CHAPTER 9
COMMONALITY — 35

CHAPTER 10
READY — 37

CHAPTER 11
LIFE-ALTERING — 39

CHAPTER 12
DESIRE — 41

CHAPTER 13
WIN THY HEART — 43

CHAPTER 14
READY OR NOT — 45

CHAPTER 15
RENDEZVOUS — 47

CHAPTER 16
BUCKET LIST — 49

CHAPTER 17
SYNCHRONICITY — 51

CHAPTER 18
DARK HOT CHOCOLATE — 53

CHAPTER 19
FIRST SIGHT — 55

CHAPTER 20

HELLO	57
CHAPTER 21 MISSING PIECE	59
CHAPTER 22 DANCE FLOOR	61
CHAPTER 23 ALBATROSS	63
CHAPTER 24 DIVINE	65
CHAPTER 25 RAINS	67
CHAPTER 26 OSCILLATORY	69
CHAPTER 27 HALO	71
CHAPTER 28 UNIVERSE	73
CHAPTER 29 OPPOSITES	75
CHAPTER 30 KISMET	77
	79

Experience

Song Title: Giver

Artist: Módl

She desired to experience God through her love.

God wanted to experience itself.

God orchestrated a chance encounter.

Feeling

Song Title: Kiss me

Artist: Frank Walker

'Where to miss?'

She whispered, 'to the feeling of seeing rain drops falling on my face',

And he leaned in for a kiss.

Moments

Song Title: Heartbeats

Artist: José Gonzales

The moments leading up to

the first intimate handheld,

every chat,

every talk,

every gaze shared

is a slice of

heaven in progress.

Instincts

Song Title: And Then Came Spring

Artist: AsWeKeepSearching

Love is so instinctual,

it might just happen

with the feeling of

that someone out there

without

even meeting them yet.

Chosen

Song Title: Infinity

Artist: James Young

'It isn't random', she believed.

At the same time somewhere,

he iterated in his mind,

'We are chosen'.

The Wait

Song Title: I love you baby

Artist : Surf Mesa feat. Emilee

It could be slow, or rather the wait seems endless.

But it could also be in an instant.

A ravishing, all consuming, ennnnnergy.

Let's leave it at that 🔥

Longing

Song Title: Lying in the Hands of God

Artist: Dave Matthews Band

She was the calm.

He was surrounded by a hundred things to do, people to meet.

He longed for the serenity that only she was, for him.

Both looked at each other

and smiled ☺

Story

Song Title: Love From NGC 7318

Artist: Barnes Blvd. · Tanerélle

She longed for that one moment where their story would start.

He felt a calling to msg her.

He slid into her dm ☺

Commonality

Song Title: Take Mine

Artist: Peter Katz

Both knew they had histories.

Both were hurt.

That was their common point.

This was the beginning of their

forever.

Ready

Song Title: See You

Artist: Christopher Bear

She was slightly distressed.

No matter what she did, she couldn't find a connection and comfort with a prospect.

Little did she know, he was readying himself to find her.

The next instant, her inbox read,

'Maybe we could catch up for a coffee or a meal if you comfortable'.

Life-Altering

Song Title: On Our Knees

Artist: Konoba feat. R.O

He took a sip waiting for her, in the humdrum of life.

He didn't know what was to come.

When he saw her entering,

his eyes froze on her every single gesture.

He knew this evening was going to

be life-changing!

Desire

Song Title: Higher Than The Mountains

Artist: Sam Garrett

He desired a feeling that would shake his existence.

He did not want to be vocal about it. But he desired it nonetheless.

A feeling higher than the mountains.

A feeling of contentment and satiety.

'Does it even exist?' he asked himself.

On the other side, she woke up with someone's answered prayer.

Win Thy Heart

Song Title: As It Was

Artist: Aime Simon (Harry Styles Cover)

She was annoyed they couldn't meet.

She decided she's not going to reply for sometime to show she was displeased.

He sent a cute bigg sorry emoji,

the next instant she said

'Okay, I understand'.

Ready Or Not

Song Title: Love Is Still The Answer

Artist: Jason Mraz

It always comes unexpectedly, banging on the door.

Such that you cannot ignore it's calling.

Rest every noise fades.

Whether you want it or not, ready or not,

you'll be lucky when it

strikes.

Rendezvous

Song Title: Again

Artist: Sasha Sloan

It was destined.

It was written.

They thought they had control over their rendezvous,

Her and his story was not even in their own hands.

Bucket List

Song Title: Coastline

Artist: Módl

They danced on the shoreline.

He took her hand and made her swirl.

She smiled and couldn't stop.

He knew he didn't want her to.

What he didn't know was,

he was unknowingly ticking off her

bucket list.

Synchronicity

Song Title: Do You Know

Artist: Henry Green

Could they have been more in sync, she wondered.

He confirmed her unsaid thought,

by enclosing her in an even tight embrace.

She smiled as they spoke without words.

Dark Hot Chocolate

Song Title: Stay Alive

Artist: José González

She was like a breath of fresh air.

He felt adrift in life.

She took a chance and ordered a dark hot chocolate for him.

When he joined her at the cafe,

He knew his hope was revived.

First Sight

Song Title: Ice

Artist: Pablo Nouvelle

Dressed in excitement.

Her: Sandals, nope, sexy heels and a bodycon dress worn.

Him: Crisp shirt and jeans put on. Cologne worn.

Were they ready for the date! Hell yes.

Was it love at first sight?

More like fusion at first sight!

Hello

Song Title: All I Need

Artist: Pablo Nouvelle feat. Lulu James

Rains pouring, breezy, a slow burning restless feeling.

She contemplated and finally sent a msg, "Voice call?"

and then immediately unsent it.

He smiled,

realising her shyness and confused state.

Next instant, her inbox beeped with a call.

She knew and he knew.

There was a blushed smile on her end and a laughter on his;

instead of a hello.

Missing Piece

Song Title: Brand New Love

Artist: Chase Eagleson

There was a rhythm, an effortlessness,

a continuous flow to their talks,

no end no beginning,

one interlaced with the other.

Both on the dinner table, her wondering where the hell he was, her entire life, her missing puzzle piece.

He uttered out loud, perhaps by mistake, 'game over';)

They laughed.

Dance Floor

Song Title: Hold On

Artist: Pablo Nouvelle feat. James Gruntz

Both had a thing for dancing!

They swirled, like ebb and flow,

energies syncing.

She set the floor on fire, he ravished it.

For anyone who saw them dancing that night,

knew they had found a partner for life!

Albeit through dancing ;)

Albatross

Song Title: It's Always Been You

Artist: Phil Wickham

'I waited and waited, but you never came.

Now you show up, where have you been all this time?', she whispered.

He said, 'It took me a long time, but I was getting ready to meet you.

Every day, every breath, prepared us for this moment.

You do not see?'

'I always believed I would find you my Albatross', she delightedly uttered.

This was

The happy ending and beginning of their love story.

Divine

Song Title: Joy In The Morning (Worship Version)

Artist: Tauren Wells

Breath to my body

Illumination to my soul

Moon to my starless night

Sunbeam to my cold skin

Fire to my moth

Music to my words

Heart to my heart

Divinity to my divinity,

Love to my pleasure,

Zeal to my life

Always to my now

Ring to my finger.

She dreamed about this poem.

On waking up in the morning, he asked her out for a dinner date!

She beamed,

Joy is on the horizon !

Rains

Song Title: Feel Good Inc

Artist: Gorillaz Chase Eagleson

Smell of first rains,

ohh smell of first rains, can anything beat that? She marvelled.

She very well knew what could beat that!

His scent,

their coffee conversations,

listening to songs together,

wonderstruck at art,

him playing her favourite song on his guitar.

She knew Petrichor would come second and,

by a longggg shot!

Oscillatory

Song Title: As It Was

Artist: Harry Styles (Loop Cover by Loopink)

The simplicity in her, the passion in her,

the excitement and wonder she beheld, was just not containable.

He didn't want to contain it,

never.

He spurred on with her energy,

like she was a clock key to his rhythm.

Both were oscillating,

And how!

Halo

Song Title: Halo (Beyonce Cover)

Artist: Peter Katz

It was undeniable for him.

She had her guards up,

but for him it was like a foregone conclusion.

Like gravity can't forget to make a fall.

She was his saving grace. His guardian angel.

Let's cross that bridge, he decided.

Somewhere, a bud blossomed!

Universe

Song Title: This Universe

Artist: Singh Kaur

'What is enlightenment?', she asked

'It is a momentous experience of heaven…, umm, okay fine, it is

undefinable', he replied with a laugh

'I liked the first part of it', she said 'momentous experience of heaven; that's very well explained'.

'What is love?', she asked

'You.., umm, okay, fine.. that is not definable either. Do you now, like the first part as well?

They just had a hearty, knowing shared giggle.

Opposites

Song Title: Wish You Were Here

Artist: Pablo Nouvelle feat. Rio

Who is this girl! I have to know her. I have to meet her.

She seems so different from me.

But that is not going to stop me from asking her out.

If they say opposites attract,

this is the

epitome of an example.

Kismet

Song Title: You And Me

Artist: Matthew Barber

They were people watching in between sips of coffee.

The corner table at the cafe was just perfect.

Everything about that evening was.

The song 'You and Me' playing in the background,

the light rains.

They didn't need words for that evening.

The vibes were conversing.

The smiles gave it all away.

Their universes were collapsing,

timelines shifting in the backdrop,

unknown to them,

Destinies were being written

What an incredible journey it has been to write this book!

To you, my dear reader, I extend my heartfelt gratitude. Thank you for embarking on this adventure with me, for turning these pages and allowing my words to transport you to new realms of imagination.

Please share your views with me and tag me on my

Instagram page *@theconscious_creator* and *@bluerose_publishers*

With heartfelt appreciation,
Henal Chokshi

www.ingramcontent.com/pod-product-compliance
Lightning Source LLC
LaVergne TN
LVHW061600070526
838199LV00077B/7119